THIS CRUISE JOURNAL BELONGS TO:

CRUISE SAVINGS

WE'RE SAVING FOR:

AMOUNT NEEDED:

OUR GOAL DATE:

DEPOSIT TRACKER

AMOUNT DEPOSITED: **DATE DEPOSITED:**

$

$

$

$

$

$

$

$

$

$

CRUISE SAVINGS

DEPOSIT TRACKER

AMOUNT DEPOSITED: **DATE DEPOSITED:**

$

$

$

$

$

$

$

$

$

$

$

$

$

CRUISE SAVINGS

DEPOSIT TRACKER

AMOUNT DEPOSITED: **DATE DEPOSITED:**

$

$

$

$

$

$

$

$

$

$

$

$

$

CRUISE SAVINGS

DEPOSIT TRACKER

AMOUNT DEPOSITED: **DATE DEPOSITED:**

$

$

$

$

$

$

$

$

$

$

$

$

$

CRUISE SAVINGS

DEPOSIT TRACKER

AMOUNT DEPOSITED:	DATE DEPOSITED:
$	
$	
$	
$	
$	
$	
$	
$	
$	
$	
$	
$	
$	

CRUISE DETAILS

NOTES

TO DO:

CRUISE DETAILS & REMINDERS:

CRUISE COUNTDOWN

MONTH: _____   YEAR: _____

M	T	W	T	F	S	S

FLIGHT INFORMATION

DATE:	DESTINATION:

AIRLINE:	
BOOKING NUMBER:	
DEPARTURE DATE:	
BOARDING TIME:	
GATE NUMBER:	
SEAT NUMBER:	
ARRIVAL / LANDING TIME:	

DATE:	DESTINATION:

AIRLINE:	
BOOKING NUMBER:	
DEPARTURE DATE:	
BOARDING TIME:	
GATE NUMBER:	
SEAT NUMBER:	
ARRIVAL / LANDING TIME:	

TRAVEL EXPENSES

BUDGET AND RECORD LOG

AMOUNT: PURPOSE:

$

$

$

$

$

$

$

$

$

$

$

$

$

CRUISE PACKING CHECKLIST

CLOTHING	✓	ESSENTIALS	✓

CRUISE PACKING CHECKLIST

CLOTHING FOR HER	✓	CLOTHING FOR HIM	✓

ESSENTIALS	✓	FOR THE JOURNEY	✓
		IMPORTANT DOCUMENTS	✓

CRUISE PACKING CHECKLIST

CLOTHING FOR HER	✓	CLOTHING FOR HIM	✓
T-Shirts &, Tank Tops & Blouses		T-Shirts & Tank Tops	
Sundresses		Shorts	
Flip Flops, Sandals & Heels		Swim Wear	
Shorts & Pants		Jeans, Khakis	
Swimsuit & Cover Up		Formal Attire (dress shirt, shoes, etc.)	
T-Shirts &, Tank Tops & Blouses		Belt	
Aqua/Swimming Shoes		Tie	
Bras, Panties & Socks		Sandals / Sneakers	
Sunhat		Visor, Baseball Cap	
Sunglasses		T-Shirts &, Tank Tops & Blouses	
Formal Attire		Sunglasses	
Jewelry		Socks & Underwear	
ESSENTIALS	✓	**FOR THE JOURNEY**	✓
Lanyard		Carry On Bag	
Suntan Lotion		Cash / Local Currency	
Medication (motion sickness, etc.)		Credit Cards	
Travel Mug / Water Bottle		Phone Charger	
		Backpack	
		IMPORTANT DOCUMENTS	✓
		Passport & ID	
		Cruise Documents & Boarding Pass	
		Flight Information	

CRUISE EXCURSION PLANNER

ACTIVITY / EXCURSION OVERVIEW:

EST COST OF EXCURSION:

INCLUSIONS:	✓	**EXCLUSIONS:**	✓
FOOD & DRINK:	☐		☐
TRANSPORTATION:	☐		☐
GRATITUTY:	☐		☐

ACTUAL COST:

IMPORTANT INFORMATION:

CONTACT: PHONE #:

MEET UP TIME: WHAT TO BRING:

ADDRESS:

CRUISE EXCURSION PLANNER

ACTIVITY / EXCURSION OVERVIEW:

EST COST OF EXCURSION:

INCLUSIONS:	✓	**EXCLUSIONS:**	✓
FOOD & DRINK:	☐		☐
TRANSPORTATION:	☐		☐
GRATITUTY:	☐		☐

ACTUAL COST:

IMPORTANT INFORMATION:

CONTACT: PHONE #:

MEET UP TIME: WHAT TO BRING:

ADDRESS:

CRUISE EXCURSION PLANNER

ACTIVITY / EXCURSION OVERVIEW:

EST COST OF EXCURSION:

INCLUSIONS:	✓	**EXCLUSIONS:**	✓
FOOD & DRINK:	☐		☐
TRANSPORTATION:	☐		☐
GRATITUTY:	☐		☐

ACTUAL COST:

IMPORTANT INFORMATION:

CONTACT: PHONE #:

MEET UP TIME: WHAT TO BRING:

ADDRESS:

CRUISE EXCURSION PLANNER

ACTIVITY / EXCURSION OVERVIEW:

EST COST OF EXCURSION:

INCLUSIONS:	✓	**EXCLUSIONS:**	✓
FOOD & DRINK:	☐		☐
TRANSPORTATION:	☐		☐
GRATITUTY:	☐		☐

ACTUAL COST:

IMPORTANT INFORMATION:

CONTACT: PHONE #:

MEET UP TIME: WHAT TO BRING:

ADDRESS:

CRUISE PORT PLANNER

DESTINATION:	DATE:

THINGS TO DO / SEE:

☐
☐
☐
☐
☐
☐
☐

WHERE TO EAT:

☐
☐
☐
☐
☐
☐
☐

TRANSPORTATION DETAILS:

☐
☐
☐
☐
☐

OTHER INFORMATION:

☐
☐
☐
☐
☐

RETURN TO SHIP BY:

CRUISE PORT PLANNER

DESTINATION:	DATE:

THINGS TO DO / SEE:

☐
☐
☐
☐
☐
☐
☐

WHERE TO EAT:

☐
☐
☐
☐
☐
☐
☐

TRANSPORTATION DETAILS:

☐
☐
☐
☐
☐

OTHER INFORMATION:

☐
☐
☐
☐
☐

RETURN TO SHIP BY:

CRUISE PORT PLANNER

DESTINATION: DATE:

THINGS TO DO / SEE:

- ☐
- ☐
- ☐
- ☐
- ☐
- ☐
- ☐

WHERE TO EAT:

- ☐
- ☐
- ☐
- ☐
- ☐
- ☐
- ☐

TRANSPORTATION DETAILS:

- ☐
- ☐
- ☐
- ☐
- ☐

OTHER INFORMATION:

- ☐
- ☐
- ☐
- ☐
- ☐

RETURN TO SHIP BY:

CRUISE PORT PLANNER

DESTINATION:	DATE:

THINGS TO DO / SEE:

☐
☐
☐
☐
☐
☐
☐

WHERE TO EAT:

☐
☐
☐
☐
☐
☐
☐

TRANSPORTATION DETAILS:

☐
☐
☐
☐
☐

OTHER INFORMATION:

☐
☐
☐
☐
☐

RETURN TO SHIP BY:

ALL ABOARD!

PRE-CRUISE TO DO LIST & CHECKLIST

1 MONTH BEFORE

2 WEEKS BEFORE

1 WEEK BEFORE

2 DAYS BEFORE

24 HOURS BEFORE

DAY OF TRAVEL

CRUISE PLANNER

WEEK OF:

MONDAY	TUESDAY	WEDNESDAY	THURSDAY
TO DO	TO DO	TO DO	TO DO
MEALS	MEALS	MEALS	MEALS

FRIDAY	SATURDAY	SUNDAY	NOTES
TO DO	TO DO	TO DO	
MEALS	MEALS	MEALS	MEALS

CRUISING TO DO LIST

CRUISE BUCKET LIST

PLACES I WANT TO VISIT:

THINGS I WANT TO SEE:

TOP 3 DESTINATIONS:

CRUISE ITINERARY

Monday

Tuesday

Wednesday

Thursday

Friday

Saturday

Sunday

CRUISE OVERVIEW

MONTH:

MONDAY	TUESDAY	WEDNESDAY	THURSDAY	FRIDAY	SATURDAY	SUNDAY

CRUISE ACTIVITIES

WEEKLY ACTIVITY TRACKER:

	M	T	W	T	F	S	S
	○	○	○	○	○	○	○
	○	○	○	○	○	○	○
	○	○	○	○	○	○	○
	○	○	○	○	○	○	○
	○	○	○	○	○	○	○
	○	○	○	○	○	○	○
	○	○	○	○	○	○	○
	○	○	○	○	○	○	○
	○	○	○	○	○	○	○
	○	○	○	○	○	○	○
	○	○	○	○	○	○	○
	○	○	○	○	○	○	○
	○	○	○	○	○	○	○
	○	○	○	○	○	○	○

DAILY ACTIVITY PLANNER

DAILY ITINERARY

ACTIVITY: _____

TIME: _____

LOCATION: _____

WEATHER: ☀ ⛅ 🌦 ☁ ⛈

MEAL PLANNER

DAILY EXPENSES

_____ _____

_____ _____

_____ _____

_____ _____

_____ _____

TOTAL COST: [   ]

TOP ACTIVITIES

TIME:	SCHEDULE:

NOTES:

DAILY ACTIVITY PLANNER

DAILY ITINERARY

ACTIVITY: ....

TIME: ....

LOCATION: ....

WEATHER:

TOP ACTIVITIES

MEAL PLANNER

TIME:	SCHEDULE:

DAILY EXPENSES

TOTAL COST:

NOTES:

DAILY ACTIVITY PLANNER

DAILY ITINERARY

ACTIVITY: _____

TIME: _____

LOCATION: _____

WEATHER: ☀️ ⛅ 🌦️ ☁️ ⛈️

MEAL PLANNER

DAILY EXPENSES

_____ _____

_____ _____

_____ _____

_____ _____

_____ _____

TOTAL COST: [   ]

TOP ACTIVITIES

TIME:	SCHEDULE:

NOTES:

DAILY ACTIVITY PLANNER

DAILY ITINERARY

ACTIVITY: _____

TIME: _____

LOCATION: _____

WEATHER: ☀ ⛅ 🌦 ☁ ⛈

MEAL PLANNER

DAILY EXPENSES

_____   _____

_____   _____

_____   _____

_____   _____

TOTAL COST: [   ]

TOP ACTIVITIES

TIME:	SCHEDULE:

NOTES:

DAILY ACTIVITY PLANNER

DAILY ITINERARY

ACTIVITY: _____

TIME: _____

LOCATION: _____

WEATHER: ☀ ⛅ 🌦 ☁ ⛈

MEAL PLANNER

TOP ACTIVITIES

TIME: SCHEDULE:

DAILY EXPENSES

_____   _____

_____   _____

_____   _____

_____   _____

_____   _____

TOTAL COST: [_____]

NOTES:

DAILY ACTIVITY PLANNER

DAILY ITINERARY

ACTIVITY: _____

TIME: _____

LOCATION: _____

WEATHER: ☀ ⛅ 🌦 ☁ ⛈

MEAL PLANNER

TOP ACTIVITIES

TIME:	SCHEDULE:

DAILY EXPENSES

TOTAL COST: [   ]

NOTES:

CRUISE FRIENDS

FRIENDS ARE FOREVER

NAME:

PHONE NUMBER:

ADDRESS:

CABIN #:

FRIENDS ARE FOREVER

NAME:

PHONE NUMBER:

ADDRESS:

CABIN #:

FRIENDS ARE FOREVER

NAME:

PHONE NUMBER:

ADDRESS:

CABIN #:

FRIENDS ARE FOREVER

NAME:

PHONE NUMBER:

ADDRESS:

CABIN #:

There's Nothing Like Cruising Life!

CRUISE FRIENDS

NAME:

PHONE NUMBER:

ADDRESS:

CABIN #:

NAME:

PHONE NUMBER:

ADDRESS:

CABIN #:

NAME:

PHONE NUMBER:

ADDRESS:

CABIN #:

NAME:

PHONE NUMBER:

ADDRESS:

CABIN #:

There's Nothing Like Cruising Life!

CRUISE FRIENDS

FRIENDS ARE FOREVER

NAME:

PHONE NUMBER:

ADDRESS:

CABIN #:

FRIENDS ARE FOREVER

NAME:

PHONE NUMBER:

ADDRESS:

CABIN #:

FRIENDS ARE FOREVER

NAME:

PHONE NUMBER:

ADDRESS:

CABIN #:

FRIENDS ARE FOREVER

NAME:

PHONE NUMBER:

ADDRESS:

CABIN #:

There's Nothing Like Cruising Life!

CRUISE FRIENDS

FRIENDS ARE FOREVER

NAME:

PHONE NUMBER:

ADDRESS:

CABIN #:

FRIENDS ARE FOREVER

NAME:

PHONE NUMBER:

ADDRESS:

CABIN #:

FRIENDS ARE FOREVER

NAME:

PHONE NUMBER:

ADDRESS:

CABIN #:

FRIENDS ARE FOREVER

NAME:

PHONE NUMBER:

ADDRESS:

CABIN #:

There's Nothing Like Cruising Life!

MY CRUISE AGENDA

MY CRUISE AGENDA

IMPORTANT CONTACTS

DOCTOR

NAME:

PHONE NUMBER:

ADDRESS:

EMAIL:

HOUSESITTER

NAME:

PHONE NUMBER:

ADDRESS:

EMAIL:

PET BOARDING

NAME:

PHONE NUMBER:

ADDRESS:

EMAIL:

EMERGENCY CONTACT

NAME:

PHONE NUMBER:

ADDRESS:

EMAIL:

TIME TO TURN ON CRUISE CONTROL!

MY CRUISE JOURNAL

DATE:

What I Did Today:

Highlight of the Day:

Thoughts & Reflections:

MY CRUISE JOURNAL

DATE:

What I Did Today:

Highlight of the Day:

Thoughts & Reflections:

MY CRUISE JOURNAL

DATE:

What I Did Today:

Highlight of the Day:

Thoughts & Reflections:

MY CRUISE JOURNAL

DATE:

What I Did Today:

Highlight of the Day:

Thoughts & Reflections:

MY CRUISE JOURNAL

DATE:

What I Did Today:

Highlight of the Day:

Thoughts & Reflections:

MY CRUISE JOURNAL

DATE:

What I Did Today:

Highlight of the Day:

Thoughts & Reflections:

MY CRUISE JOURNAL

DATE:

What I Did Today:

Highlight of the Day:

Thoughts & Reflections:

CRUISE SAVINGS

WE'RE SAVING FOR:

AMOUNT NEEDED:

OUR GOAL DATE:

$

DEPOSIT TRACKER

AMOUNT DEPOSITED: **DATE DEPOSITED:**

$

$

$

$

$

$

$

$

$

$

CRUISE SAVINGS

DEPOSIT TRACKER

AMOUNT DEPOSITED: **DATE DEPOSITED:**

$

$

$

$

$

$

$

$

$

$

$

$

$

CRUISE SAVINGS

DEPOSIT TRACKER

AMOUNT DEPOSITED: **DATE DEPOSITED:**

$

$

$

$

$

$

$

$

$

$

$

$

$

CRUISE SAVINGS

DEPOSIT TRACKER

AMOUNT DEPOSITED: **DATE DEPOSITED:**

$

$

$

$

$

$

$

$

$

$

$

$

$

CRUISE SAVINGS

DEPOSIT TRACKER

AMOUNT DEPOSITED:　　　　　　　　　　　**DATE DEPOSITED:**

$

$

$

$

$

$

$

$

$

$

$

$

$

CRUISE DETAILS

NOTES

TO DO:

CRUISE DETAILS & REMINDERS:

CRUISE COUNTDOWN

MONTH: _____   YEAR: _____

M	T	W	T	F	S	S

FLIGHT INFORMATION

DATE:	DESTINATION:

AIRLINE:	
BOOKING NUMBER:	
DEPARTURE DATE:	
BOARDING TIME:	
GATE NUMBER:	
SEAT NUMBER:	
ARRIVAL / LANDING TIME:	

DATE:	DESTINATION:

AIRLINE:	
BOOKING NUMBER:	
DEPARTURE DATE:	
BOARDING TIME:	
GATE NUMBER:	
SEAT NUMBER:	
ARRIVAL / LANDING TIME:	

TRAVEL EXPENSES

AMOUNT:　　　　　　　　　　　　　　　　**PURPOSE:**

$

$

$

$

$

$

$

$

$

$

$

$

$

CRUISE PACKING CHECKLIST

CLOTHING	✓	ESSENTIALS	✓

CRUISE PACKING CHECKLIST

CLOTHING FOR HER	✓	CLOTHING FOR HIM	✓

ESSENTIALS	✓	FOR THE JOURNEY	✓

		IMPORTANT DOCUMENTS	✓

CRUISE PACKING CHECKLIST

CLOTHING FOR HER	✓	CLOTHING FOR HIM	✓
T-Shirts &, Tank Tops & Blouses		T-Shirts & Tank Tops	
Sundresses		Shorts	
Flip Flops, Sandals & Heels		Swim Wear	
Shorts & Pants		Jeans, Khakis	
Swimsuit & Cover Up		Formal Attire (dress shirt, shoes, etc.)	
T-Shirts &, Tank Tops & Blouses		Belt	
Aqua/Swimming Shoes		Tie	
Bras, Panties & Socks		Sandals / Sneakers	
Sunhat		Visor, Baseball Cap	
Sunglasses		T-Shirts &, Tank Tops & Blouses	
Formal Attire		Sunglasses	
Jewelry		Socks & Underwear	
ESSENTIALS	✓	**FOR THE JOURNEY**	✓
Lanyard		Carry On Bag	
Suntan Lotion		Cash / Local Currency	
Medication (motion sickness, etc.)		Credit Cards	
Travel Mug / Water Bottle		Phone Charger	
		Backpack	
		IMPORTANT DOCUMENTS	✓
		Passport & ID	
		Cruise Documents & Boarding Pass	
		Flight Information	

CRUISE EXCURSION PLANNER

ACTIVITY / EXCURSION OVERVIEW:

EST COST OF EXCURSION:

INCLUSIONS:	✓	**EXCLUSIONS:**	✓
FOOD & DRINK:	☐		☐
TRANSPORTATION:	☐		☐
GRATITUTY:	☐		☐

ACTUAL COST:

IMPORTANT INFORMATION:

CONTACT: PHONE #:

MEET UP TIME: WHAT TO BRING:

ADDRESS:

CRUISE EXCURSION PLANNER

ACTIVITY / EXCURSION OVERVIEW:

EST COST OF EXCURSION:

INCLUSIONS: ✓

FOOD & DRINK: ☐

TRANSPORTATION: ☐

GRATITUTY: ☐

EXCLUSIONS: ✓

☐

☐

☐

ACTUAL COST:

IMPORTANT INFORMATION:

CONTACT: PHONE #:

MEET UP TIME: WHAT TO BRING:

ADDRESS:

CRUISE EXCURSION PLANNER

ACTIVITY / EXCURSION OVERVIEW:

EST COST OF EXCURSION:

INCLUSIONS:	✓	**EXCLUSIONS:**	✓
FOOD & DRINK:	☐		☐
TRANSPORTATION:	☐		☐
GRATITUTY:	☐		☐

ACTUAL COST:

IMPORTANT INFORMATION:

CONTACT: PHONE #:

MEET UP TIME: WHAT TO BRING:

ADDRESS:

CRUISE EXCURSION PLANNER

ACTIVITY / EXCURSION OVERVIEW:

EST COST OF EXCURSION:

INCLUSIONS:	✓	**EXCLUSIONS:**	✓
FOOD & DRINK:	☐		☐
TRANSPORTATION:	☐		☐
GRATITUTY:	☐		☐

ACTUAL COST:

IMPORTANT INFORMATION:

CONTACT: PHONE #:

MEET UP TIME: WHAT TO BRING:

ADDRESS:

CRUISE PORT PLANNER

DESTINATION: DATE:

THINGS TO DO / SEE:

☐
☐
☐
☐
☐
☐
☐

WHERE TO EAT:

☐
☐
☐
☐
☐
☐
☐

TRANSPORTATION DETAILS:

☐
☐
☐
☐
☐

OTHER INFORMATION:

☐
☐
☐
☐
☐

RETURN TO SHIP BY:

CRUISE PORT PLANNER

DESTINATION: DATE:

THINGS TO DO / SEE:

☐
☐
☐
☐
☐
☐
☐

WHERE TO EAT:

☐
☐
☐
☐
☐
☐
☐

TRANSPORTATION DETAILS:

☐
☐
☐
☐
☐

OTHER INFORMATION:

☐
☐
☐
☐
☐

RETURN TO SHIP BY:

CRUISE PORT PLANNER

DESTINATION:	DATE:

THINGS TO DO / SEE:

☐
☐
☐
☐
☐
☐
☐

WHERE TO EAT:

☐
☐
☐
☐
☐
☐
☐

TRANSPORTATION DETAILS:

☐
☐
☐
☐
☐

OTHER INFORMATION:

☐
☐
☐
☐
☐

RETURN TO SHIP BY:

CRUISE PORT PLANNER

DESTINATION:	DATE:

THINGS TO DO / SEE:

☐
☐
☐
☐
☐
☐
☐

WHERE TO EAT:

☐
☐
☐
☐
☐
☐
☐

TRANSPORTATION DETAILS:

☐
☐
☐
☐
☐

OTHER INFORMATION:

☐
☐
☐
☐
☐

RETURN TO SHIP BY:

ALL ABOARD!

PRE-CRUISE TO DO LIST & CHECKLIST

1 MONTH BEFORE

2 WEEKS BEFORE

1 WEEK BEFORE

2 DAYS BEFORE

24 HOURS BEFORE

DAY OF TRAVEL

CRUISE PLANNER

WEEK OF:

MONDAY	TUESDAY	WEDNESDAY	THURSDAY
TO DO	TO DO	TO DO	TO DO
MEALS	MEALS	MEALS	MEALS

FRIDAY	SATURDAY	SUNDAY	NOTES
TO DO	TO DO	TO DO	
MEALS	MEALS	MEALS	MEALS

CRUISING TO DO LIST

CRUISE BUCKET LIST

PLACES I WANT TO VISIT:

THINGS I WANT TO SEE:

TOP 3 DESTINATIONS:

CRUISE ITINERARY

Monday

Tuesday

Wednesday

Thursday

Friday

Saturday

Sunday

CRUISE OVERVIEW

MONTH:

MONDAY	TUESDAY	WEDNESDAY	THURSDAY	FRIDAY	SATURDAY	SUNDAY

CRUISE ACTIVITIES

WEEKLY ACTIVITY TRACKER:

	M	T	W	T	F	S	S
	○	○	○	○	○	○	○
	○	○	○	○	○	○	○
	○	○	○	○	○	○	○
	○	○	○	○	○	○	○
	○	○	○	○	○	○	○
	○	○	○	○	○	○	○
	○	○	○	○	○	○	○
	○	○	○	○	○	○	○
	○	○	○	○	○	○	○
	○	○	○	○	○	○	○
	○	○	○	○	○	○	○
	○	○	○	○	○	○	○
	○	○	○	○	○	○	○
	○	○	○	○	○	○	○
	○	○	○	○	○	○	○

DAILY ACTIVITY PLANNER

DAILY ITINERARY

ACTIVITY: _____

TIME: _____

LOCATION: _____

WEATHER:

MEAL PLANNER

TOP ACTIVITIES

TIME:	SCHEDULE:

DAILY EXPENSES

_____   _____

_____   _____

_____   _____

_____   _____

TOTAL COST: [   ]

NOTES:

DAILY ACTIVITY PLANNER

DAILY ITINERARY

ACTIVITY: _____

TIME: _____

LOCATION: _____

WEATHER: ☀️ ⛅ 🌦️ ☁️ ⛈️

MEAL PLANNER

TOP ACTIVITIES

TIME:	SCHEDULE:

DAILY EXPENSES

TOTAL COST: [   ]

NOTES:

DAILY ACTIVITY PLANNER

DAILY ITINERARY

ACTIVITY: _____

TIME: _____

LOCATION: _____

WEATHER: ☀ ⛅ 🌦 ☁ ⛈

MEAL PLANNER

TOP ACTIVITIES

TIME:	SCHEDULE:

DAILY EXPENSES

_____ _____

_____ _____

_____ _____

_____ _____

TOTAL COST: [   ]

NOTES:

DAILY ACTIVITY PLANNER

DAILY ITINERARY

ACTIVITY: _____

TIME: _____

LOCATION: _____

WEATHER: ☀ ⛅ 🌦 ☁ ⛈

MEAL PLANNER

TOP ACTIVITIES

TIME:	SCHEDULE:

DAILY EXPENSES

_____ _____

_____ _____

_____ _____

_____ _____

_____ _____

TOTAL COST: [_____]

NOTES:

DAILY ACTIVITY PLANNER

DAILY ITINERARY

ACTIVITY: ....

TIME: ....

LOCATION: ....

WEATHER: ☀ ⛅ 🌦 ☁ ⛈

MEAL PLANNER

TOP ACTIVITIES

TIME:	SCHEDULE:

DAILY EXPENSES

TOTAL COST: [   ]

NOTES:

DAILY ACTIVITY PLANNER

DAILY ITINERARY

ACTIVITY: _____

TIME: _____

LOCATION: _____

WEATHER: ☀ ⛅ 🌦 ☁ ⛈

MEAL PLANNER

TOP ACTIVITIES

TIME: SCHEDULE:

DAILY EXPENSES

_____   _____

_____   _____

_____   _____

_____   _____

_____   _____

TOTAL COST: [_____]

NOTES:

CRUISE FRIENDS

NAME:

PHONE NUMBER:

ADDRESS:

CABIN #:

NAME:

PHONE NUMBER:

ADDRESS:

CABIN #:

NAME:

PHONE NUMBER:

ADDRESS:

CABIN #:

NAME:

PHONE NUMBER:

ADDRESS:

CABIN #:

There's Nothing Like Cruising Life!

CRUISE FRIENDS

FRIENDS ARE FOREVER

NAME:

PHONE NUMBER:

ADDRESS:

CABIN #:

FRIENDS ARE FOREVER

NAME:

PHONE NUMBER:

ADDRESS:

CABIN #:

FRIENDS ARE FOREVER

NAME:

PHONE NUMBER:

ADDRESS:

CABIN #:

FRIENDS ARE FOREVER

NAME:

PHONE NUMBER:

ADDRESS:

CABIN #:

There's Nothing Like Cruising Life!

CRUISE FRIENDS

FRIENDS ARE FOREVER

NAME:

PHONE NUMBER:

ADDRESS:

CABIN #:

FRIENDS ARE FOREVER

NAME:

PHONE NUMBER:

ADDRESS:

CABIN #:

FRIENDS ARE FOREVER

NAME:

PHONE NUMBER:

ADDRESS:

CABIN #:

FRIENDS ARE FOREVER

NAME:

PHONE NUMBER:

ADDRESS:

CABIN #:

There's Nothing Like Cruising Life!

CRUISE FRIENDS

FRIENDS ARE FOREVER

NAME:

PHONE NUMBER:

ADDRESS:

CABIN #:

FRIENDS ARE FOREVER

NAME:

PHONE NUMBER:

ADDRESS:

CABIN #:

FRIENDS ARE FOREVER

NAME:

PHONE NUMBER:

ADDRESS:

CABIN #:

FRIENDS ARE FOREVER

NAME:

PHONE NUMBER:

ADDRESS:

CABIN #:

There's Nothing Like Cruising Life!

MY CRUISE AGENDA

MY CRUISE AGENDA

IMPORTANT CONTACTS

DOCTOR

NAME:

PHONE NUMBER:

ADDRESS:

EMAIL:

HOUSESITTER

NAME:

PHONE NUMBER:

ADDRESS:

EMAIL:

PET BOARDING

NAME:

PHONE NUMBER:

ADDRESS:

EMAIL:

EMERGENCY CONTACT

NAME:

PHONE NUMBER:

ADDRESS:

EMAIL:

TIME TO TURN ON CRUISE CONTROL!

MY CRUISE JOURNAL

DATE:

What I Did Today:

Highlight of the Day:

Thoughts & Reflections:

MY CRUISE JOURNAL

DATE:

What I Did Today:

Highlight of the Day:

Thoughts & Reflections:

MY CRUISE JOURNAL

DATE:

What I Did Today:

Highlight of the Day:

Thoughts & Reflections:

MY CRUISE JOURNAL

DATE:

What I Did Today:

Highlight of the Day:

Thoughts & Reflections:

MY CRUISE JOURNAL

DATE:

What I Did Today:

Highlight of the Day:

Thoughts & Reflections:

MY CRUISE JOURNAL

DATE:

What I Did Today:

Highlight of the Day:

Thoughts & Reflections:

MY CRUISE JOURNAL

DATE:

What I Did Today:

Highlight of the Day:

Thoughts & Reflections:

Made in United States
North Haven, CT
26 January 2023

31516172R00057